THE POETRY AND THE EVOLUTION OF COMPASSION

PROFESSOR PATRICK PIETRONI

FRESCO BOOKS

CONTENTS

No.	281685	Sex M	C.N PATRICK	S.N PIETRONI
Code			Father C.N MICHAEL	S.N PIETRONI
			Nionality BRIT. SUB.	Race CYPRIOT OTHER
			Birthplace LIMASSOL	Date of Birth 8 NOV 42
			Occupation PUPIL	R.T.P.
			Address CATERINA KORNAKOU 1 NICOSIA	
Interviewing clerk or agent's signature, seal and date of issue Halydoros			R.O. or A.R.O's signature, seal and date of issue	

EVOLUTION AND IDENTITY

Born in Cyprus
Small Island in the Mediterranean
Part of the British Empire.

Four Grandparents
All different nationalities
Identity Card says
CYPRIOT-OTHER

Seeking safety
Decided British was best
Sang Rule Britannia
Joined the British Army

4

Woke up one day
And added R to evolution.

Now smoke a pipe (English)
Drink Ricard (French)
Eat Feta and olives (Greek)
Love Opera (Italian)
Sabbatical in Cincinnati (America)
Lived in Ashram (Namaste)

Still time to discover more
And evolve into what?
A gardener of my
Inherited seeds and
Discovered loves.

Some Great Thinker Wrote
An interpenetrating harmonious mix up.

No need for the
Tyranny of one identity

Learn to live with the wound
Of not knowing who you are.
But continue to discover
Who you can become.

Patrick Pietroni [1]

INTRODUCTION

The first five volumes of this series covered:
Vol. I   The Poetry of Compassion
Vol. II   Poetry and the Science of Compassion
Vol. III The Poetry of Global Compassion
Vol. IV Poetry and the Education of Compassion
Vol. V   Poetry and the Psychology of Compassion

The framework of these short volumes is to allow the reader to have an introduction to the specific focus of the book, which is accompanied by poems and images that help to add an aesthetic and emotional experience.

This particular volume focusses on the evolution of compassion and tries to bring together two of the most contested subjects in academia. The debates have generated hundreds, if not thousands of academic papers and learned books, and I make no pretence or indeed attempt to cover this vast area, but hope, dear reader, you will be stimulated enough to pursue your own further exploration of these debates.

THE EVOLUTIONARY DEBATES

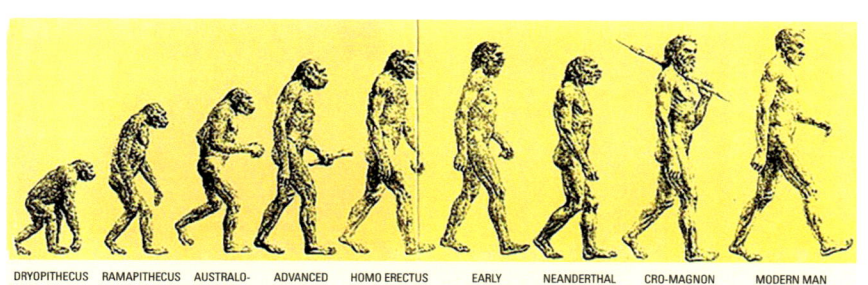

| DRYOPITHECUS (14-8 million yrs.) | RAMAPITHECUS (12-8 million yrs.) | AUSTRALO-PITHECUS (4 million yrs.) | ADVANCED AUSTRALO-PITHECUS (2 million yrs.) | HOMO ERECTUS (1.8-0.3 million yrs.) | EARLY HOMO SAPIENS (400,000-100,000 yrs.) | NEANDERTHAL MAN (150,000-30,000 yrs.) | CRO-MAGNON MAN 130,000-60,000 yrs.) | MODERN MAN (40,000 yrs. to present) |

OUR PRESENT TIME PERSPECTIVE

Big Bang (formation of universe)	1 January
Formation of Earth	14 September
Origin of life	25 September
Significant oxygen	1 December
First fish	19 December
First mammals	26 December
First humans	31 December
First cave painting	11:59 pm
Christ	11:59:56 pm
Renaissance	11:59:59 pm
Present day	First second of New Year's Day

As the above two diagrams illustrate the "modern human species" is a very late outcome on the planet earth. Homo sapiens has evolved from a long line of previous species, and it was Charles Darwin's original work that was the first scientific attempt to explore how this came about. It is Darwin's detailed study of fossils and the emerging academic discipline of geology that laid the groundwork for all future discoveries. It was Darwin's detailed study of pigeon skulls, the English fantail and the scorpion fish, which persuaded him that there was a progressive fossil record that supported his theory of evolution. He may also have been influenced by his grandfather Erasmus Darwin who wrote the following poem:

THE TEMPLE OF NATURE (extract)

Organic life beneath the shoreless waves
Was born and nurs'd in Ocean's pearly caves;
First forms minute, unseen by spheric glass,
Move on the mud, or pierce the watery mass:
These, as successive generations bloom,
New powers acquire, and larger limbs assume;
Whence countless groups of vegetation spring,
And breathing realms of fin and feet and wing.

Erasmus Darwin [2]

John van Wyke in his article Darwin vs God [3] writes:

The immensely ancient Earth was not Darwin's contribution, and it was not new. Geology had become a sophisticated science. No one knew how old the Earth was, but it was clear from the enormous numbers of geological formations that had been described and classified that so many long ages must have taken unimaginable lengths of time, millions upon millions of years. But no one knew how many. It was not until the discovery of radioactivity that accurate dating of rocks, and of the Earth itself, were feasible. [4]

The fossil discoveries and the geologic strata in which they were found allowed for a sequencing i.e. shells, fish, amphibians, reptiles, mammals, and the most important implication was that the appearance of the human species was a very new occurrence. It was clear that if God had created the Earth he did not do it in seven days.

These debates of the origin of the earth and man continue to this day between Creationists (intelligent design) and Modern Darwinians. We will return to this debate later. Darwin proposed in his two books *On the Origin of the Species* [5] and *The Descent of Man* [6] that evolution occurs over decades, centuries and millennia through a process of natural selection. Matt Ridley, in his ambitious book *The Evolution of Everything* [7] writes,

Human society evolves. Change in technology, language, morality and society is incremental, inexorable, gradual and spontaneous. It follows a narrative, going from one stage to the next; it creeps rather than jumps, it has its own spontaneous momentum rather than being driven from outside; it has no goal or end in mind; and it largely happens by trial and error – a version of natural selection. Much of the human world is the result of human action, but not of human design: it emerges from the interactions of millions, not from the plans of a few. [8]

This view is controversial as we shall encounter in the section on Social Evolution. Before then we need to return to Image 2 and trace the evolution of the brain, mind, consciousness and free-will. These areas of studies allow us to have a greater understanding of the evolution of compassion, or as Darwin wrote,

We are ... impelled to relieve the sufferings of another, in order that our own painful feelings may be at the same time relieved. In like manner we are led to participate in the pleasures of others.

Sympathy beyond the confines of man, that is, humanity to the lower animals, seems to be one of the latest moral acquisitions.... This virtue, one of the noblest with which man is endowed, seems to arise incidentally from our sympathies becoming more tender and more widely diffused, until they are extended to all sentient beings. [9]

EVOLUTION AND THE HUMAN BRAIN

The "triune brain", as first described by Paul Mclean,[10] and made popular by Carl Sagan in his ground-breaking book *The Dragons of Eden*,[11] is no longer considered to be as definite as first described. Nevertheless, it provides a helpful description of the evolution of the mammalian brain. This model suggests the following and is illustrated below:

Reptilian brain — governing our basic instincts
Limbic system — governing our emotional experience and behaviour
Neocortex — governing our thoughts, language and judgement

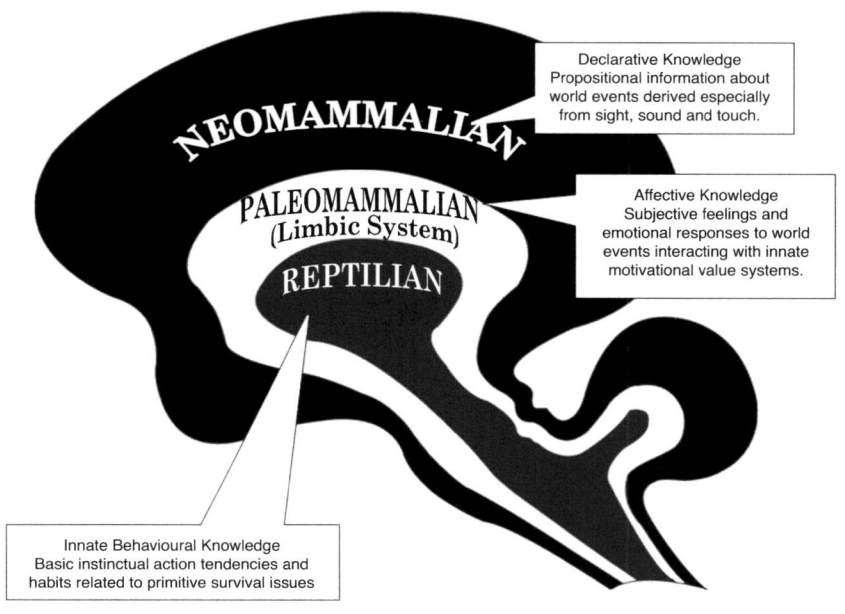

NEOMAMMALIAN

PALEOMAMMALIAN
(Limbic System)

REPTILIAN

Declarative Knowledge
Propositional information about world events derived especially from sight, sound and touch.

Affective Knowledge
Subjective feelings and emotional responses to world events interacting with innate motivational value systems.

Innate Behavioural Knowledge
Basic instinctual action tendencies and habits related to primitive survival issues

DEAR BRAIN

You fold up my memories
like origami cranes
hide them in secret pockets
tuck them in boxes upstairs
and I never know which ones
you will give me back in dreams.

Like a carrier pigeon
you bring messages
back and forth
            left to right
whispering to yourself
and I hear you, for I am you.

Today I think I am writing a poem
but you are the one holding the pen
you are the one shaking my head
you are the one crossing out words
choosing just what and what not
I (who am you) should say.

Amy Ludwig VanDerwater [12]

The Reptilian Brain — allows us to control body temperature, blood pressure, breathing, sleep and other basic functions.

The Limbic Structures — regulates some of our instinctual responses and emotions e.g. fear, anger, stress regulation and social emotions, including love and hate.

The Neocortex — is the most recent development of the brain; with its two hemispheres it provides us with what we could call "our brain". Thinking, reflection, consciousness, judgement and the ability to influence and modify the functions of the limbic system and our instinctual responses.

Paul Gilbert in his book *The Compassionate Mind* [13] summarises the evolution of our brain as follows:

> *Something happened in the evolution of the human mind a few million years ago that made our minds radically different to those of other species. Actually scientists don't think it was one thing that happened but a series of interconnected adaptions. Humans eventually evolved into the primate who remains dependent the longest with a brain maturation process that far exceeds that of all other species.*
>
> *The human brain starts out about the same size as a chimpanzee's, 350cc, but during its first four years of development, it will triple in size, then grow more slowly until it reaches around 1,500cc. Not only is there a rapid increase in size post-birth, but there is also considerable development in the branching and connecting-up of neurons (nerve cells). In the first years of life, the human brain undergoes a radical transformation as millions upon millions of new connections are formed and laid*

down in increasingly complex networks day by day. The maturing, branching, networking and organizing trajectories of the brain give rise to increasingly complex potentials for thinking, feeling and behaving in a multiplicity of social ways. Two key processes direct these abilities: the genes we are born with and our experiences in life. When some event occurs, the brain responds and neurons fire in complex patterns like fireworks. When they do they start connecting to each other. A well-known finding suggests that 'neurons that fire together wire together'. So you can imagine how extensively the brain of an infant receiving soothing and affection will be getting wired up compared to one of an infant receiving little soothing, who is also neglected or often being stressed. [14]

Arthur Koestler in his book, *Janus* [15] suggested that there is a basic fault in the way the human brain evolved. He suggested that the neuronal connection between the neo-cortex and the limbic structures and the reptilian brain are not "fit for purpose". He likened it to a rider trying to control a wild horse without any reins. That our evolved brain may have faulty wiring may help to explain much of human behaviour we find difficult to control.

GENES – NATURAL SELECTION
AND SEXUAL SELECTION

HEREDITY

I am the family face;
Flesh perishes, I live on,
Projecting trait and trace
Through time to times anon,
And leaping from place to place
Over oblivion.

The years-heired feature that can
In curve and voice and eye
Despise the human span
Of durance — that is I;
The eternal thing in man,
That heeds no call to die.

Thomas Hardy [16]

WHAT'S UP WITH DNA?

DNA is built to divide.
It passes its code, it's designed to survive.
You get half from your mother
and half from your father;
with DNA we receive the tools to be alive.
DNA is made of two antiparallel strands.
Base pairs join them like two lightly clasped hands.
The expression of a gene can influence
how you handle the milk of a Holstein.
Lactose intolerance could make you
change your dessert plans.
DNA can predict the color of your hair.
DNA can influence whether you sneeze
when you see the sun's glare.
Through science and sharing
all of our DNA comparing.
We can learn more about ourselves
and become aware!

Mason LaMarche [17]

It has to be remembered that Darwin developed his theory of evolution through natural selection well before the discovery of genes and the essential part they play in who we are and who we can become. Genes are the basic building blocks that we inherit from our parents that provide the map that will determine the design of our bodies, our brains and most everything else. This genetic potential is known as our genotype. However, our external environment experience both in the womb and throughout our life will influence our inherited genotype and is known as our phenotype, e.g. if you have inherited genes which allow you to become six feet tall, you may, if you are born in America become a world-class basketball player. If you were born in a country that doesn't play basketball that achievement will not be possible. So, yes, our inherited genes (our genotype) are the "design" but our diverse experience (our phenotype) could be viewed as the designer, often now referred to as the epi-genetic factor. Darwin, without knowing anything about genotypes and phenotypes, built the theory of evolution through natural selection following his meticulous study of the fossil remains of plants, birds, animals and human remains.

Natural Selection

Darwin returned from his second voyage of the Beagle in 1836 and had accumulated the evidence that was to propel him to formulate his theory of natural selection.

What Darwin did was to formulate how these progressive changes occurred i.e. from shellfish to mammals to Homo sapiens. What created the major controversy at the time and still persists to this day was that he labelled the process "natural selection" i.e., there was no external "creator" involved. Darwin wrote:

If during the long course of ages and under varying conditions of life, organic beings vary at all in the several parts of their organisation, and I think this cannot be disputed; if there be, owing to the high geometrical powers of increase of each species, at some age, season, or year, a severe struggle for life, and this certainly cannot be disputed; then, considering the infinite complexity of the relations of all organic beings to each other and to their conditions of existence, causing an infinite diversity in structure, constitution, and habits, to be advantageous to them, I think it would be a most extraordinary fact if no variation ever had a code useful to each being's own welfare, in the same way as so many variations have occurred useful to man. But if variations useful to any organic being do occur, assuredly individual cells characterised will have the best chance of being preserved in the struggle for life; and from the strong principle of inheritance they will tend to produce offspring similarly characterised. This principle of preservation, I have called, for the sake of brevity Natural Selection.[18]

Although hotly disputed at the time, Darwin summarises his theory of evolution by natural selection as "the principle by which each slight variation (of a trait) if useful is preserved". Herbert Spencer, a contemporary of Darwin's, coined the term "the survival of the fittest",[19] and this has, unfortunately become the shorthand description for Darwin's theory. It is more accurate to describe Darwin's theory of evolution as the survival of those who can adapt. This more accurately captures the reality of the evidence and is exemplified by Darwin's quote:

Sympathy beyond the confines of man, that is humanity to the lower animals, seems to be one of the latest moral acquisitions. ... This virtue, one of the noblest with which man is endowed, seems to arise incidentally from our sympathies becoming more tender and more widely diffused, until they are extended to all sentient beings.[20]

The survival of the fittest is the ageless law of nature.

but the fittest are rarely the strong.

The fittest are those endowed with the qualifications for
adaptation, the ability to accept the inevitable and
conform to the unavoidable, to harmonize with
existing or changing conditions.

Dave E Smalley

NATURAL SELECTION

The gradual but inexorable magic
That turned the dinosaurs into the birds
Had no overt, only a hidden, logic.
To start the squadrons climbing from the herds
No wand was ever waved, but afterwards
Those who believed there must have been a wizard
Said the whole show looked too well-planned for hazard.

And so it does, in retrospect. Such clever
Transitions, intricate beyond belief!
The little lobsters, in their mating fever,
Assaulted from the sea, stormed up the cliff,
And swept inland as scorpions. But if
Some weapons freak equipped their tails for murder
He must have thought sheer anguish all in order.

Source of all good and hence of evil, pleasure
And hence of pain, he is, or else they are,
Without a moral sense that we can measure,
And thus without a mind. Better by far
To stand in awe of blind chance than to fear
A conscious mechanism of mutation
Bringing its fine intentions to fruition

Without a qualm about collateral horror.
The peacock and the tapeworm both make sense.
Nobody calls the ugly one an error.
But when a child is born to pain intense
Enough to drive its family all at once
To weep blood, an intelligent designer
Looks like a torture garden's beaming owner.

No, give it up. The world demands our wonder
Solely because no feeling brain conceived
The thumb that holds the bamboo for the panda.
Creation, if the thing's to be believed —
And only through belief can life be loved —
Must do without that helping hand from Heaven.
Forget it, lest it never be forgiven.

Clive James [21]

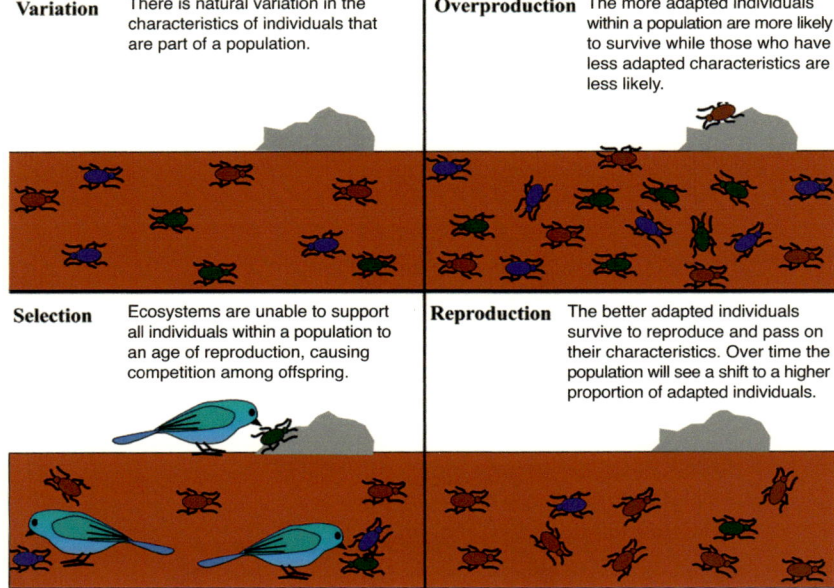

Variation There is natural variation in the characteristics of individuals that are part of a population.

Overproduction The more adapted individuals within a population are more likely to survive while those who have less adapted characteristics are less likely.

Selection Ecosystems are unable to support all individuals within a population to an age of reproduction, causing competition among offspring.

Reproduction The better adapted individuals survive to reproduce and pass on their characteristics. Over time the population will see a shift to a higher proportion of adapted individuals.

However, given how "survival of the fittest" is so often linked incorrectly to Darwin's theory, it is important to unpack the term "fittest". — The assumption is often made that survival of the fittest implies survival of the strongest. It, of course, could also refer to survival of the kindest. So how do we determine what is the "fit" that is required for the species to ensure its survival?

We are living through a pandemic (at the time of writing this book) caused by a very tiny virus which is challenging not only our health services, but has also made us increasingly aware that the populations that have most suffered include the most vulnerable in the United States: Black, Hispanic, Native Americans, those in elderly care homes, those compromised by the conditions linked to poverty (diabetes, obesity, mental health) and those who have been forgotten – inmates of our prisons. We are yet to arrive at a consensus as to how best to respond to this crisis (I outline this challenge we face in great detail in the third volume of this series on Global Compassion [22]).

I also make the point that this current threat from the Covid-19 pandemic must be viewed, terrible as it is, as a dress rehearsal for the many challenges, perils and threats that are to come from the consequences of climate change. We will be challenged to consider whether in this crisis "the survival of the fittest" will imply "the strongest", or whether "fittest" will involve the "survival of the kindest".

Peter Kropotkin in his book *Mutual Aid: A Factor of Evolution* [23] presented mutual aid as one of the dominant factors of evolution, the other being self-assertion, and concluded that,

In the practice of mutual aid, which we can retrace to the earliest beginnings of evolution, we thus find the positive and undoubted origin of our ethical conceptions; and we can affirm that in the ethical progress of man, mutual support not mutual struggle has had the leading part. In its wide extension, even at the present time, we also see the best guarantee of a still loftier evolution of our race. [24]

We shall return to the application of this moral theory in the section on social evolution.

Sexual Selection

Darwin felt from the very beginning that his theory of evolution by natural selection did not sufficiently explain all that he had observed and collected. He, together with Russel Wallace, conceived of sexual selection as sufficiently different from natural selection to require a separate designation. He outlined how the process of sexual selection i.e. the mating encounter involved male-male competition as well as female choice. He writes:

[Sexual Selection] depends, not on a struggle for existence, but on a struggle between the males for possession of the females; the result is not death to the unsuccessful competitor, but few or no offspring.

... when the males and females of any animal have the same general habits of life, but differ in structure, colour, or ornament, such differences have been mainly caused by sexual selection.[27]

Darwin's theory of sexual selection was not initially accepted, or indeed, understood. It took the work of the biologist Sir Ronald Fisher [28] and more recent research by William Donald Hamilton[29] and others who now form what has become known as the Third Darwin Revolution or Modern Darwinism.

Sexual selection has been observed in many different species including birds, reptiles, amphibians, insects, spiders and humans. Intra-sexual selection occurs as male-male competition (rutting stags) where the strongest does win. Females select by trait e.g. length of male tail (peafowl), colourful plume (bird-of-paradise).

THE SURVIVAL OF THE FITTEST
IS THE AGELESS LAW OF NATURE

The survival of the fittest is the ageless law of nature,
but the fittest are rarely the strong.
The fittest are those endowed with
the qualifications for adaptation,
the ability to accept the inevitable
and conform to the unavoidable,
to harmonize with existing or changing conditions.

Dave E Smalley [25]

THEIR BLACK HEARTS

All the traps are placed from the jealous people in my life
Still trying to fight all the battles of their unwanted strife

All the things I have to lose as I am made to take the fall
Because; have we all not met before, so jealous if I recall

I am still visiting the graves of loved ones who fell before
Now I'm back to try for them, and even the bloody score

All died from your jealousy; under, an accidental disguise
With all their deaths forever noted by all the judges wise

Staying put to calm your jealous hearts was, but; a farce
As all it did was fuel the jealously within your black hearts

You still killed the ones I loved so you could rest assured
Never questioning once the pain that for you we endured

Survival of the fittest, as with all of your righteous rights
Saving me creeping upon you all, in your sleepless nights.

Indiana Shaw [26]

THE ANTHROPOCENE AND ITS
EVOLUTIONARY CONSEQUENCES

James Joyce wrote that human beings were a "... parenthesis of infinitesimal brevity."

It was only when geology and the study of identifying and naming different rock formations and fossilised remains that we began to understand the origin of our universe, i.e. planet earth is 4.5 billion years old and homo sapiens – and modern humans emerged in Africa about 50,000 years ago. More recently geologists have argued intensively over the term "The Anthropocene" – at what point in time did the human species begin to have real impact on Mother Earth. Some have chosen 1850 or so, with the beginning of the Industrial Revolution in England (fossil fuels, coal mines, electricity, etc). Others prefer 1945, with the explosion of nuclear bombs.

Several of the seminal books that were written in the Sixties "Limits to Growth", "Population Bomb", "Only One Earth" appeared to portray such a bleak picture and many of their wilder predictions were so patently wrong that for a while their warnings and suggested solutions were ridiculed and disregarded.

Recently similar books with more up to date scientific analysis have propelled a more acute and universal attempt to address this "climate change crisis". Naomi Klein's "This Changes Everything", Al Gore's two books, "An Inconvenient Truth" and "An Inconvenient Sequel" have propelled the debate to be heard almost daily and is now fully supported by the United Nations. The emergence of Greta Thunberg and

Donald Trump have helped to ensure the debate will receive the attention on social media. [30]

In the booklet *The Poetry of Global Compassion* [31] I outlined the impact "climate change" was having on our environment — the sea, the forests, the climate, the air we breathe and the water we drink. Only in the last decade have we begun to explore the evolutionary effects of human actions on not only human but nonhumans as well. The word "Anthropocene" was first included in the Oxford Dictionary in June 2014. The term "Plastacene" was also considered as plastics were taken to be a marker for the beginning of the Anthropocene. Philip Larkin wrote, "What will survive of us is love".[32] It is more likely that what will survive is plastic and lead-207, the stable isotope linked to the uranium-235 decay chain.

In 2010 Timothy Morton adopted the term hyperobject to denote some of the characteristic entities of the Anthropocene. Hyperobjects are "so massively distributed in time, space and dimensionality" that they defy our perception, let alone our comprehension. Among the examples Morton gives of hyperobjects are climate change, mass species extinction and radioactive plutonium. "In one sense [hyperobjects] are abstractions," he notes, "in another they are ferociously, catastrophically real." [33]

To this list we can now add "pandemic":

Thinking about both humans and nonhumans within this kind of evolutionary and ethical framework allows us to address basic questions about different conservation scenarios. Should we abandon attempts at biodiversity conservation?

This scenario would mean pursuing a human evolutionary trajectory that ignores nonhumans in a blind Anthropocene — a choice sure to have many unintended consequences (11).

What we conserve defines what we are or pretend to be. We must establish and promote comprehensive dialogs among social scientists, ecologists, and evolutionary biologists to explore the biological and cultural roots of our interactions with nonhumans and to understand the origins of our inertia in the face of the urgency of biodiversity erosion. Addressing this major challenge for humanity may also enhance our ability to respect each other in our societies.[34]

SOCIAL EVOLUTION AND HUMAN BEHAVIOUR

The principles of social evolution, sometimes labelled "modern Darwinism", are linked to the work of W.D. Hamilton and can be both complex and difficult to comprehend. I have found it helpful to begin with a description of General Systems Theory and George Engel's application of this to medicine and healthcare.

General Systems Theory

Paul Weiss[35] and Ludwig Von Bertalanffy,[36] who are credited with the first exposition of what is now known as General Systems Theory, were biologists who were not afraid to draw on computer and engineering insights in trying to understand their own discipline of biology. Their model of examining the world involved the recognition that nothing could be studied on its own and everything was part of a system.

A system consists of objects with properties which cohere. The relationships that are brought about by this coherence not only tie the system together, but create conditions from which the properties arise. The importance of the concept of a system is that within an environment a set of objects can be seen to cohere and interact in such a way that their attributes define the nature of the system, and may create properties which the system alone manifests. The coming together to form a system is called systematisation and any tendency of the objects to fall apart is called segregation. [37]

George Engel, [38] the foremost physician to utilise General Systems Theory, advocated a break from the traditional biomedical model with its emphasis on reductionistic and mechanistic thinking that underpins much of the most recent medical advance. Engel labelled his approach to medicine, biopsycho-social and contrasted this with the bio-medical model, which he saw as the predominant "folk-medicine" of Western society. He saw the need to abandon this model as it failed to explain and, more importantly, treat a large proportion of the "dis-eases" and illnesses that beset western man.

Engel drew heavily on Systems Theory to explain and expand on the biopsycho-social approach. He drew on Weiss's statement that nature is ordered both as a hierarchy and a continuum. The components of these models were each given the distinction of a "system". Each system or level in the hierarchy possessed distinct characteristics of its own, i.e. a cell operates very differently from a person. — Yet each system is a component that can operate as a dynamic whole, but at the same time is a component of a higher system, e.g. a cell is part of a tissue and tissues form organs, etc. Thus, each system is both a "whole" and at the same time forms part of a greater whole.

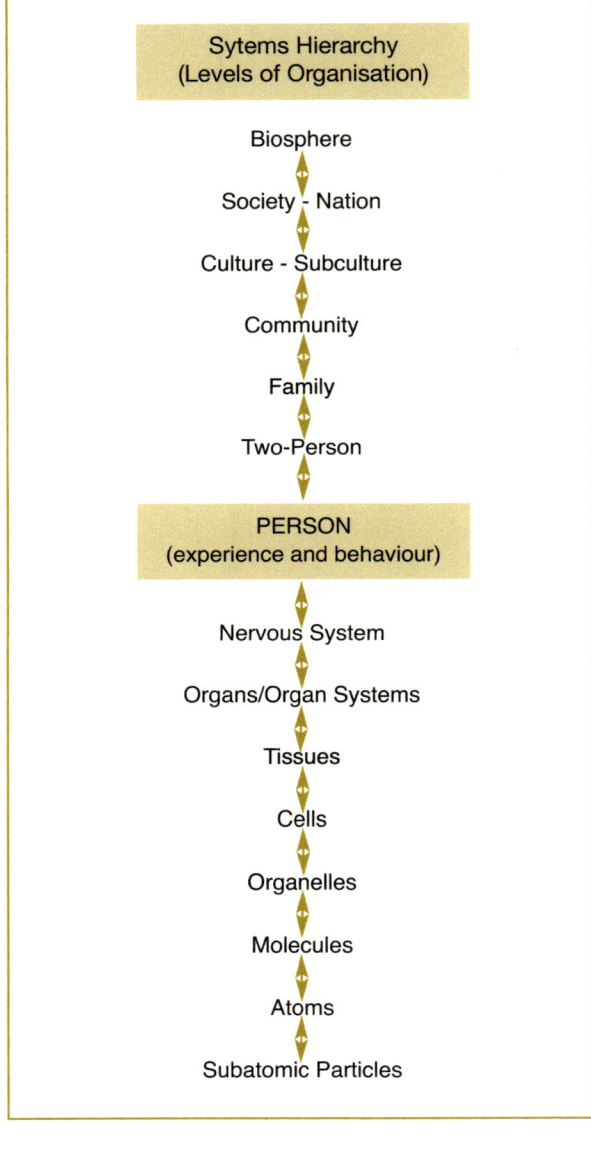

**Sytems Hierarchy
(Levels of Organisation)**

Biosphere

Society - Nation

Culture - Subculture

Community

Family

Two-Person

**PERSON
(experience and behaviour)**

Nervous System

Organs/Organ Systems

Tissues

Cells

Organelles

Molecules

Atoms

Subatomic Particles

EVOLUTIONARY BIOLOGY

In *Principles of Social Evolution* [39] Andrew Bourke writes,

> *Principles of Social Evolution demonstrate how social evolution lies at the heart of the history of life.* [40]

He continues,

> *I take the view that a fundamental problem posed by the evolution of cooperation has been solved by Hamilton's (1964) inclusive fitness theory. Hamilton's (1964) theory solved it through the insight, later expanded by Dawkins selfishness at the level of genes. When an organism exhibits self-sacrificial behaviour, it does so because a gene for self-sacrifice is levering its way into the next generation either through enhancing the future reproduction of its current bearer (direct benefit, as in narrow-sense cooperation) or through promoting aid to relatives that bear the same gene (indirect or kin-selected benefit, as in altruism). Hence, from the viewpoint of the focal gene, there is selection for maximizing transmission to future generations, just as Darwinian natural selection leads us to expect. It follows that, despite occasional claims to the contrary, the evolution of cooperation is no longer quite the fundamental challenge to natural selection theory that it once seemed.* [41]

W D Hamilton

- Leading authority in the world of kin selection
- Used inclusive finess to support theory
- Inspired by Haldane, and RA Fisher
- His rule RB > C explains when altruism would continue
- R = how related the animals are (brother vs cousin, etc)
- B = benefit to group (inclusive fitness)
- C = cost to individual (loss of individual fitness

DARWIN: EMPATHY, ALTRUISM AND COMPASSIONATE SYMPATHY

The challenge in discussing this topic is often one of definition, and even when these terms are defined, there seems so much overlap that confusion may still remain. Rather than summarise these terms from the extensive literature that exists I prefer to share with you my own understanding:

You are in a pub/bar on a hot summer day and are about to order a drink. You hear the pub door swing open and a man staggers in drenched in sweat. He is dressed indicating he has just run a marathon. He looks at you and says, "Sorry, I have no money":

Sympathy is if you say, "Don't worry, I will buy you one"

Empathy	is when you see his sweaty face, you say, "You are making me feel thirsty as well. I will buy myself the same drink"
Compassion	is after you both have finished your drinks you say, "My car is outside, can I give you a lift somewhere?"
Kindness	is not minding when he vomits all over your car because you bought him a very cold pint of light beer when he had asked for some warm lemonade
Concern	is when he passes out in your car and urinates
Intelligent Kindness	is when you decide to take him to the nearest hospital
Relief	is when you arrive home and vow to not take pity on anyone again
Altruism	is what you believe your behaviour to have been
Irritation	is when your wife tells you off for sitting on the sofa with vomit all over your clothes
Anger	is what you feel when she tells you are always trying to play the Good Samaritan and that charity should begin at home
Insight	is when deep down you know she is right and that you have all too often refused to mow the lawn when she asks you to, or do the washing up
Reflection	is when you decide you will go and see a counsellor, start jogging, and you arrive at your first session having run from your home
Your Breakdown	is when the counsellor notices you are sweating and asks whether you want a drink.

So why did/does Compassion evolve in the Human Species?

Darwin in his final book, *The Descent of Man, and Selection in Relation to Sex* [42] viewed what he labelled as "sympathy" as the strongest of human's evolved instincts. He wrote:

> *... those communities, which included the greatest number of the most sympathetic members, would flourish best and rear the greatest number of offspring.* [43]

This became a contested view during his lifetime and for years to come. It was the Modern Darwinists that latterly confirmed and added to Darwin's original statement. There is now a general consensus that compassion has emerged as an "affective state" orientated to the welfare of others for three different reasons and outcomes. They are:

1. Because they enhance the welfare of vulnerable offspring
2. Because it is a positive attribute and involves the mate selection processes
3. Because it enhances and facilitates the cooperative relations with non-kin

In Compassion (an evolutionary analysis and empirical review)[44] the authors outline the supporting evidence:

> *Within the vulnerable offspring argument, compassion is thought to have emerged as the affective element of a caregiving system, designed to help raise vulnerable offspring to the age of viability (thus ensuring that genes are more likely to be replicated). Human offspring are born more prematurely and more dependent than any other mammal, requiring unprecedented care to reach the age of independence and reproductive engagement.* [45]

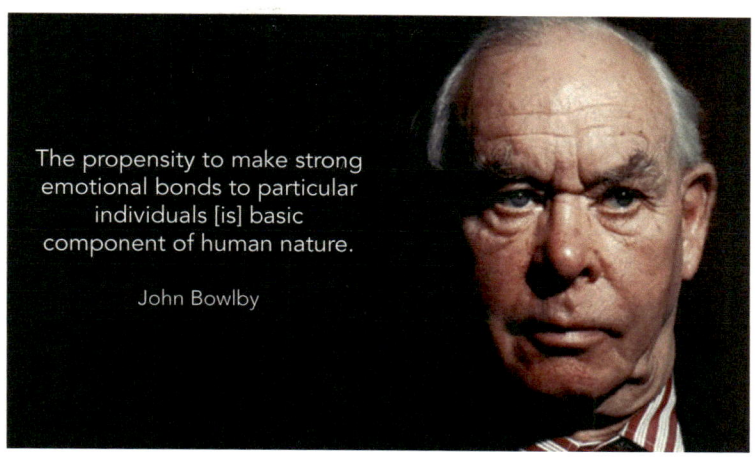

The propensity to make strong emotional bonds to particular individuals [is] basic component of human nature.

John Bowlby

John Bowlby's work on early Attachment Theory

Bowlby was born in 1907 and died in 1990. He started his life work before the Second World War and a 1940 paper, *The influence of early environment in the development of neurosis and neurotic character*,[46] already pointed to his later conclusions. He joined the staff of the Tavistock Clinic after the war and held various senior posts there, where he latterly forged links with many workers in anthropology and ethology. He published his main findings in the three-volume work: Attachment and Loss series: *Attachment; Separation: Anxiety and Anger; and Loss: Sadness and Depression*. [47] His later books included *The Making and Breaking of Affectional Bonds* [48] and *A Secure Base: Clinical Application of Attachment Theory*. [49] Just before he died, he finished a biography of Charles Darwin, [50] which is an essay in applied Bowlbyism. This quote illustrates the simplicity and common-sense nature of the man:

There are few blows to the human spirit so great as the loss of someone near and dear. Traditional wisdom knows that we can be crushed by grief and die of a broken heart, and also that a jilted lover is apt to do things that are foolish and dangerous to himself and others. It knows too that neither love nor grief is felt for just any other human being, but only for one, or a few particular and individual human beings. The core of what I term 'affectional bond' is the attraction that one individual has for another individual. [51]

Drawing on many studies, Bowlby illustrates how "anxious attachment" occurs in children after a separation from mother or mother figure and as a result of parental desertion and divorce. He links anxious attachment to the development of anxiety, phobias and insecurity in childhood and adult life. Bowlby contrasted "anxious attachment" with "secure attachment", and believed:

There is a strong case for believing that an unthinking confidence in the unfailing accessibility and support of attachment figure is the bedrock on which stable and self-reliant personality is built. [51]

Other authors write,

A second evolutionary argument for the emergence of compassion is found within sexual selection theory, which details the processes by which certain traits are selected for through the mate preferences of females and males (Buss & Kenrick, 1998; Miller, 2007). Here the focus is on compassion as a trait like tendency to feel the emotion and to act altruistically. The benefits to reproducing with compassionate individuals are clear, as intimated in Darwin's early analysis. More inclined to feel compassion during times of others' need and suffering, compassionate reproductive partners should be more likely to devote more resources to offspring, to provide physical care—protection, affection, and touch—and to create cooperative, caring communities so vital to the survival of offspring. [52]

Compassion enhances and facilitates the cooperative relation with non-kin. In the first introductory booklet I contrasted proximal compassion towards our kin (it is the first syllable in kindness) to this third evolutionary theorising as with the concept of distal compassion.

Distal compassion captures how we respond to something we see on television or read in the newspaper or hear on the radio. Darwin wrote:

We are ... impelled to relieve the sufferings of another, in order that our own painful feelings may be at the same time relieved.

... a civilized man, or even boy, who never before risked his life for another, but full of courage and sympathy, has disregarded the instinct of self-preservation and plunged at once into a torrent to save a drowning man, though a stranger. [53]

This third non-kin emergence of compassion is best summarised as follows:

The implication of this third line of evolutionary argument is that individuals will favor enduring relationships with more agreeable, compassionate individuals because this emotional trait predicts increased cooperative, trustworthy behavior and mutually beneficial exchanges among individuals not bound by kin relations. Framed within this cooperative non-kin argument, it is interesting to note that children high in dispositional empathy and compassion enjoy richer friendship networks (Zhou et al., 2002); that adolescents high in self-reported agreeableness, which strongly predicts the experience of compassion (Shiota et al., 2006), have more friends and are more accepted by their peers than adolescents low in agreeableness (Jensen-Campbell et al., 2002); and that across cultures group members go to great lengths to punish individuals who are not cooperative (Henrich et al., 2006). [55]

I finish with two succinct poems:

COMPASSION IS TO CHANGE;
WHAT REVOLUTION IS TO EVOLUTION

What is compassion,
But a line than cannot be seen,
But must be crossed to be able to believe in better things.
To say I'm sorry for the crimes that one shall commit,
Time and time again,
Is what it means to begin at the end.
With self-reflect comes self-correct and this shall bring an era of
self-respect.

P0r5h4n4 R33d 55

ANY ORDINARY FAVOUR WE DO

An ordinary favor we
do for someone or any
compassionate reaching out
may seem to be going nowhere
at first, but may be planting
a seed we can't see right now.
Sometimes we need to just
do the best we can and then
trust in an unfolding
we can't design or ordain.

Sharon Salzberg [56]

References

1. Pietroni, P. (2020). *Evolution and Identity*. Unpublished.
2. Darwin, E. (1803). *The Temple of Nature or The Origin of Society*. Baltimore. John W Butler and Bonsal & Niles. Available at https://books.google.co.uk/books/about/The_Temple_of_Nature_Or_The_Origin_of_So.html?id=84AgAAAAMAAJ&printsec=frontcover&source=kp_read_button&redir_esc=y#v=onepage&q&f=false. Last accessed July 2020.
3. Wyke, J. van. (2009). Darwin vs God. *BBC History Magazine* 10, No. 1 (January): 26-31.
4. Wyke, J. van. (2009). *ibid*.
5. Darwin, C. (2004. First published 1859). *The Origin of Species by means of Natural Selection or the Preservation of Favoured Races in the Struggle for Life*. London. Castle Books.
6. Darwin, C. (2004. First published 1871). *The Descent of Man, and Selection in Relation to Sex*. Moor. J. & Desmond, A. (Eds). London. Penguin Books.
7. Ridley, M. (2015). *The Evolution of Everything: How New Ideas Emerge*. London. Fourth Estate.
8. Ridley, M. (2015). *ibid*.
9. Darwin, C. (2004. First published 1871). *op.cit*.
10. McLean, P. (1990). *The Triune Brain in Evolution: Role in Paleocerebral Functions*. New York. Springer.
11. Sagan, C. (1977). *The Dragons of Eden: Speculations on the Evolution of Human Intelligence*. New York. Radom House.
12. Ludwig VanDerwater, A. (2014). *Dear Brain*. Available at http://www.poemfarm.amylv.com/2014/10/dear-brain-free-verse-letter-poems.html Last accessed July 2020.
13. Gilbert, P. (2009). *The Compassionate Mind*. London. Constable.
14. Gilbert, P. (2009). *ibid*.

15. Koestler, A. (1983. First published 1978.). *Janus: A Summing Up*. London. Picador.

16. Hardy, T. (1917). *Heredity*. Available at https://www.poemhunter.com/poem/heredity-2/. Last accessed July 2020.

17. LaMarche, M. (2018). *What's up with DNA*. Available at https://education.23andme.com/dna-poems/. Last accessed July 2020.

18. Darwin, C. (2004. First published 1859). *op.cit.*

19. Spencer, H. (1864). *The Principles of Biology*. London. William & Norgate.

20. Darwin, C. (1871). *op.cit.*

21. James, C. (2008). *Natural Selection From Angels Over Elsinore*. London. Picador. Available at https://www.clivejames.com/natural-selection.html. Last accessed July 2020.

22. Pietroni, P. (2020). *The Poetry of Global Compassion*. Albuquerque. Fresco Books.

23. Kropotkin, P. (1914. First published 1902). *Mutual Aid: A Factor of Evolution*. London. William Heinemann.

24. Kropotkin, P. (1914. First published 1902). *ibid*.

25. Smalley, Dave E. (?) *The Survival of the Fittest is the Ageless Law of Nature*. Available at http://www.finestquotes.com/author_quotes-author-Dave+E.+Smalley-page-0.htm. Last accessed July 2020.

26. Shaw, I. (2020). *Their Black Hearts*. Available at https://www.poetrysoup.com/poem/their_black_hearts_1266090. Last accessed July 2020.

27. Darwin, C. (2004. First published 1859). *op.cit.*

28. Fisher, R. A. (1930). *The Genetical Theory of Natural Selection*. Oxford. Clarendon Press.

29. Hamilton W.D. (2002). *Narrow Roads of Gene Land Vol. 2: Evolution of Sex*. Oxford. Oxford University Press.

30. Pietroni, P. (2020). *op.cit.*

31. Pietroni, P. (2020). *op.cit.*

32. Larkin, P. An Arundel Tomb. Available at https://www.poetry foundation.org/poems/47594/an-arundel-tomb. Last accessed July 2020.

33. Macfarlane, R. Generation Anthropocene: How humans have altered the planet for ever. *The Guardian*. 1 April 2016. Available at https://www.theguardian.com/books/2016/apr/01/generation-anthropocene-altered-planet-for-ever. Last accessed July 2020.

34. Sarrazin, F. & Lecomte, J. Evolution in the Anthropocene. *Science*. 26 Feb 2016: Vol. 351, Issue 6276, pp. 922-923. Available at https://science.sciencemag.org/content/351/6276/922.full?ijkey=m3P3.FDepeGYQ&keytype=ref&siteid=sci. Last accessed July 2020.

35. Weiss, P. (1973). *The Science of Life: The living system – a system for living*. New York: Futura.

36. Von Bertalanffy, L. (1968). *General System Theory: Foundations, Development, Applications*. New York. G. Braziller.

37. Weiss, P. (1973). *op.cit.*

38. Engel, G. (1980). The Clinical Application of the Biopsychosocial Model. *The American Journal of Psychiatry* 137(5) 5 May 1980, pp. 535-544.

39. Bourke, A. (2011). *Principles of Social Evolution*. New York. Oxford University Press.

40. Bourke, A. (2011). *ibid.*

41. Bourke, A. (2011). *op.cit.*

42. Darwin, C. (2004. First published 1871). *op.cit.*

43. Darwin, C. (2004. First published 1871). *op.cit.*

44. Goetz, J. L., Keltner, D., & Simon-Thomas, E. (2010). Compassion: An evolutionary analysis and empirical review. *Psychological Bulletin*, 136(3), 351–374. Available at http://europepmc.org/article/PMC/2864937. Last accessed July 2020.

45. Goetz, J. L., Keltner, D., & Simon-Thomas, E. (2010). *ibid.*

46. Bowlby, J. (1940). The influence of early environment in the development of neurosis and neurotic character. *The International Journal of Psychoanalysis*, 21, 154–178.

47. Bowlby, J (1988). *Attachment and Loss series: Attachment; Separation: Anxiety and Anger; and Loss: Sadness and Depression.* Tavistock Professional Book. London: Routledge.

48. Bowlby, J. (1979). *The Making and Breaking of Affectional Bonds.* Abingdon. Taylor & Francis.

49 Bowlby, J. (1988). *A Secure Base: Clinical Application of Attachment Theory.* Oxon. Routledge.

50. Bowlby, J. (1991). *Charles Darwin: A New Life.* New York: Norton.

51. Bowlby, J. (1979). *op.cit.*

52. Goetz, J.L., Keltner, D., & Simon-Thomas E. (2010). *op.cit.*

53. Darwin, C. (2004. First published 1871). *op.cit.*

54. Goetz, J.L., Keltner, D., & Simon-Thomas E. (2010). *op.cit.*

55. P0r5h4n4 R33d. (?). *Compassion is to Change; What Revolution is to Evolution.* Available at https://www.poemhunter.com/poem/compassion-is-to-change-what-revolution-is-to-evolution/#content. Last accessed July 2020.

56. Salberg, S. (?). *Any ordinary favor we do.* Available at https://www.quotetab.com/quotes/by-sharon-salzberg. Last accessed July 2020.

Image Credits

Russell Good, Darwin's statue in front of Shrewsbury Library
(formerly Darwin's school), front cover
Patrick Pietroni Identity Card, p.4
Evolutionary debates – image available at http://acerzam.
blogspot.com/2016/09/evolution-of-human-stupidity.html, p.7
Our present time perspective – adapted from Sagan, C. (1977).
*The Dragons of Eden: Speculations on the Evolution of Human
Intelligence.* New York. Random House, p.7
Erasmus Darwin by Joseph Wright of Derby. Available at
https://commons.wikimedia.org/w/index.php?curid=515673, p.8
Schematic representation of hierarchical brain organisation based on
P D MacLean's triune brain concept, p.11
Cartoon of Charles Darwin as an ape. Available at https://commons.
wikimedia.org/wiki/File:Editorial_cartoon_depicting_Charles_
Darwin_as_an_ape_(1871).jpg, p.15
Image by John Tecuceanu on Unsplash. Quote available at https://
quotefancy.com/quote/1714201/Dave-Smalley-The-survival-of-
the-fittest-is-the-ageless-law-of-nature-but-the-fittest-are, p.21
Natural Selection. NicholasToal / CC BY-SA
https://creativecommons.org/licenses/by-sa/4.0, p.24
Peacock by Steve Harvey on Unsplash, p.26
Systems Hierarchy by DIISC, p.34
Image of WD Hamilton – James King-Holmes/Science Photo
Library, p.36
Image of John Bowlby available at https://en.wikipedia.org/wiki/John_Bowlby
Quote is from (1988). A Secure Base: Parent-child attachment and
healthy human development. London. Routledge, p.39

Publisher
SF Design, llc / Fresco Books
Albuquerque, New Mexico
frescobooks.com

ISBN: 978-1-934491-79-9